'N SYNC

'N SYNC

**Lexi Martin
with Jessica Davis**

Metro**Books**

Dedication

This book is dedicated to the girls who make the boy bands famous: the fans, both young and older. The former include Melissa Parnes, Courtney Vaughan-Lane, Elizabeth Iannelli, Megan Hines, Laura Miller, Desiree Adams, Amber Orick, Katie Foxton, and Amanda and Jessica Wirthlin; the latter—don't hit me—include Denise Smith, Diane Heinbokel, and Jean Wirthlin.

This book is also dedicated to a young future author—Jessica Hudson. Save me a copy of your first book!

Acknowledgments

This book could not have been completed without the assistance of my coauthor, Jessica Davis, and chief research assistant, Brittany Duncan. May the pugs be with you!

Special thanks to the Glen Este 'N SYNC research team: Ericka Heinbokel, Amanda Smith, Autumn Franz, Korie Cherry, and Amanda Middleton. Thanks also to the many 'N SYNC fans on the Web who shared their feelings and stories.

MetroBooks

An imprint of Friedman/Fairfax Publishers

©2000 by Michael Friedman Publishing Group, Inc.

Library of Congress Cataloging-in-Publication Data
Martin, Lexi.
'N Sync / Lexi Martin, with Jessica Davis.
p.cm.
includes bibliographical references and index.
ISBN 1-58663-061-X (alk. paper)
1. 'N Sync (Musical group)—Miscellanea. 2. Rock Musicians—United States—Biography. I. Davis, Jessica. II. Title.

ML421.N22 M37 2000
782.42164'2—dc21
[B]   00-032923

Editor: Ann Kirby and Dan Heend
Art Director: Jeff Batzli
Designer: Betty Found
Photography Editor: Kathleen Wolfe
Production Manager: Rosy Ngo

Color separations by Radstock Repro
Printed in England by Butler & Tanner Ltd.

3 5 7 9 10 8 6 4 2

For bulk purchases and special sales, please contact:
Friedman/Fairfax Publishers
Attention: Sales Department
15 West 26th Street
New York, NY 10010
212/685-6610 Fax 212/685-1307

Visit our website:
www.metrobooks.com

Previous pages: Strike a pose! Lookin' smooth at a 1998 photo shoot.

Above: JC, Chris, Joey, Lance, and Justin live to entertain.

Contents

'N-troducing 'N SYNC   8

CHAPTER ONE

Mouse Ears and Early Years   10
God Must Have Spent a Little More Time on 'N SYNC
Quiz: How Well Do You Know 'N SYNC by Now?

CHAPTER TWO

Chris Kirkpatrick   16
Quiz: How Well Do You Know Cool, Crazy Chris?

CHAPTER THREE

JC Chasez   26
Quiz: How Well Do You Know Jumpin', Jivin' JC?

CHAPTER FOUR

Driving the Girls Crazy   36
Giving Their All: 'N SYNC Loves Charities
Quiz: All 'N SYNC, All the Time

CHAPTER FIVE

Justin Timberlake   48
Quiz: How Well Do You Know Bouncing, Blue-eyed Justin?

CHAPTER SIX

Lance Bass   56
Quiz: How Well Do You Know Lucky, Laid-back Lance?

CHAPTER SEVEN

Diamonds Are a Band's Best Friend   64
'N SYNC's Music and Media Catalogue
Quiz: Test Your CD IQ

CHAPTER EIGHT

Joey Fatone   76
Quiz: How Well Do You Know Flirtatious, Funny Joey?

CHAPTER NINE

No Strings Attached to These Boys   84
Surfin' for 'N SYNC on the Web

Sources   92
Index   94

Right: For the girl who has everything—just put a big bow around these five guys and leave them on the front porch! (L–R, Joey, JC, Chris, Lance, and Justin)

'N-troducing 'N SYNC

What can you say about a band that has risen from obscurity to superstardom in just a few short years? You can take it for granted that the five young men who comprise the group are cute and clean cut, with just enough attitude to make young girls swoon. You could add, for the benefit of the older girls—and their moms, too—that their looks and personalities are varied enough to please anyone. From a curly-locked, baby-blue-eyed churchgoing crooner to a bold, brash Italian stallion from New York with an eye for the ladies, these guys are hot. They are no wimpy, whiny schoolboys with voices breaking, but grown-up young men not ashamed to flash their buff bods and finely honed pecs on the concert stage. (It's not just the singing the girls are screaming about, you know!)

Above and opposite: Crazy for You: 'N SYNC in New York, 1998.

Can they sing? Can ten million fans be wrong? With their first, self-titled album reaching beyond the ten million mark, and with sales of their latest CD, *No Strings Attached*, breaking all previous sales records, these guys have earned their spurs. As the latter CD's title indicates, the band recently cut the apron strings with their early management team, Lou Pearlman and his TransContinental Group, and their record company, BMG Entertainment and RCA Records. After signing with the Zomba Group's Jive Records and struggling through some bitter legal hassles, the group emerged more or less unscathed but armed with a new determination and a grittier edge. Less of a boy band, and more of a band.

'N SYNC sites litter the Internet and their faces peer out from hundreds of magazines. Is this overkill? Not to the millions of fans who can't seem to get enough. As 'N SYNC leaps into the millennium with a fifty-two-show tour (with 1 million tickets sold the first day of sale, according to *Billboard* magazine), countless television appearances, movie deals in the making, and even an Oscar nomination, there is no indication that this band has to worry about becoming a has-been any time soon. It doesn't take a psychic to predict a glittering future for the five guys in the band with the oddly punctuated name. They already have fame and fortune, millions of adoring fans, and record-breaking sales.

Maybe it's time the uninitiated gave these guys a listen—and maybe even some respect.

CHAPTER 1

Mouse Ears and Early Years

By now, all the tried-and-true 'N SYNC fans can rattle off this part of their history by heart. But record-breaking CD sales may have led some new fans into the fold, so here are some of the highlights of 'N SYNC's early years.

Chris Kirkpatrick, a native of Pittsburgh, is the acknowledged founder of 'N SYNC. A class clown in school, Chris comes from a musical family and polished his music and comedy talents by acting in school musicals such as *Oliver!* and *South Pacific*. While attending college in Florida in 1995, Chris got a job at nearby Universal Studios, singing and performing with a fifties-style doo-wop band. There he met Joey Fatone, a native New Yorker who also worked at Universal, performing with The Beetlejuice Graveyard Review.

Meanwhile, Maryland native JC Chasez was also in Orlando pursuing his own music career. After his rendition of Richard Marx's song "Right Here Waiting" earned him first place in a talent contest that he had entered on a dare, JC followed his mother's advice and auditioned for Disney's new Mickey Mouse Club (MMC) in 1991. Selected from among more than twenty thousand kids, he appeared for four years on the successful show, where other castmates included Britney Spears, Keri Russell, Christina Aguilera, Tony Luca, and a curly-haired blonde kid named Justin Timberlake.

Justin began his musical career in church back in his hometown of Memphis, Tennessee. When *Star Search* came to Memphis looking for young talent, Justin was good enough that the show's producers brought the eleven-year-old and his mother to Orlando, where the show was televised. Justin did not walk away a winner, but while he was in Orlando he learned that the producers of the new Mickey Mouse Club were going to be auditioning across the country. Shortly after returning to Memphis, he and his mother headed to

Nashville for the MMC auditions. As millions of 'N SYNC fans know, Justin was selected from more than thirty thousand kids who tried out for MMC in 1993. His family moved from Memphis to Orlando, and at age twelve Justin joined JC and the other cast members of the *New Mickey Mouse Club*. His career was short-lived, since the show was canceled in 1994, but the move would prove very significant.

The paths of the four future 'N SYNC members crossed many times before the group was formed. Justin and JC stayed in touch after MMC was canceled, and the two met Joey Fatone, who had gone to high school with some other MMC cast members. Through Joey, JC and Justin also met Chris Kirkpatrick, and the four sometimes ran into each other at vocal auditions. Chris and Joey talked it over, then Chris told Justin—who was only fourteen at the time—that he was interested in starting a band. Justin called JC, and the stage was set.

Justin's mother, Lynn Harless (she and Justin's father, Randy Timberlake, divorced many years ago), shared a house with the four boys for nearly two years, handling business issues and publicity, touring with them, and pretty much helping out with everything. Lynn's most important contribution to the group was its name. Impressed with the way their harmonies and dance steps worked together, she commented that the guys were really "in sync." The phrase had a certain ring to it, and Lynn started playing with letters to see if she could come up with a clever way of turning the phrase into some kind of acronym using the guys' names. Finally she hit on the magic combination— change the "in" to "'n" and it would work using the last letter of each boy's first name. At the time, a boy named Jason was temporarily singing the deeper vocal parts, but he stayed with the group only a short time—just long enough for the "N" at the end of his

Above: How many future famous faces can you pick out in this group shot of Disney's New Mickey Mouse Club?

Opposite: Hmmmm—can you guess which one is NOT in 'N SYNC? Justin, Lance, a familiar mouse, and Chris strike a pose behind a kneeling Joey and JC.

name to become a critical part of the "'N SYNC" moniker.

Around that time, Justin's former vocal coach recommended Mississippi-bred Lance Bass as the group's baritone. Lance never officially auditioned for the group; they simply knew right away that he was the missing link. In the group's official book, Lance recalls, "We sang 'The Star Spangled Banner' together, or something like that, and that was it." Unfortunately, since his first name ends in "E," it didn't fit the 'N SYNC acronym. But when the guys started calling him by the nickname "Lansten," everything fell into place: JustiN, ChriS, JoeY, LansteN, and JC. The final touch came when a psychic suggested that if they put a star on the cover of their debut album, it would become a hit. Just like magic, 'N SYNC was born.

'N SYNC might never have come to be if lead singers JC Chasez and Justin Timberlake hadn't met on the set of The New Mickey Mouse Club; they are pictured here during the show's fifth season.

How Well Do You Know 'N SYNC by Now?

1. Which band member is considered the founder of 'N SYNC?
a. Justin Timberlake
b. Lance Bass
c. Joey Fatone
d. Chris Kirkpatrick

2. What is JC Chasez's real first name?
a. Jared
b. Jason
c. Joshua
d. Jeremy

3. Which of the band members was the last to join 'N SYNC?
a. Justin Timberlake
b. Lance Bass
c. Joey Fatone
d. JC Chasez

4. Which band member recently started a Web site where he will soon be selling his own line of clothing?
a. Joey Fatone
b. Chris Kirkpatrick
c. Lance Bass
d. Justin Timberlake

5. Which member of 'N SYNC collects anything to do with Superman?
a. JC Chasez
b. Justin Timberlake
c. Chris Kirkpatrick
d. Joey Fatone

6. Which band member is a big fan of basketball, and a major fan of Michael Jordan?
a. Justin Timberlake
b. Joey Fatone
c. JC Chasez
d. Lance Bass

7. Which member of 'N SYNC appeared in a small role on the TV show *SeaQuest*?
a. JC Chasez
b. Chris Kirkpatrick
c. Lance Bass
d. Joey Fatone

8. Which band member's mother came up with the name 'N SYNC?
a. Chris Kirkpatrick
b. Joey Fatone
c. Justin Timberlake
d. JC Chasez

9. Which band member attended Rollins College in Orlando, Florida?
a. JC Chasez
b. Chris Kirkpatrick
c. Joey Fatone
d. Lance Bass

10. On the first leg of 'N SYNC's first American tour, they were the opening act. Later in the tour, they became the main attraction. What major performer did they open for?
a. Janet Jackson
b. Michael Jackson
c. Celine Dion
d. Shania Twain

ANSWERS
1. d 2. c 3. b 4. b 5. d 6. a
7. d 8. c 9. b 10. a

God Must Have Spent a Little More Time on 'N Sync

To really find out what makes a group tick, ask the fans. Thais Helena Antoniazi Ordine is a fan from Campinas, São Paulo, Brazil, who hopes 'N SYNC will come to Brazil someday. "I don't have a favorite member," she explains, "but what I like most about these guys is the way they fight against their problems and the way they treat their fans—they seem to really care about every single fan." Tracy Plouffe of Saco, Montana, would do more than walk a mile to see one of their smiles: "Some friends and I traveled 240 miles just to chance meeting them. We sat at the venue until the buses left, then followed after them, breaking every traffic law in Winnipeg, no doubt! . . . I am totally devoted to these guys!"

Shawnee Diana Smith of Watertown, Tennessee, remembers how she and her twin sister, Danielle, went searching for 'N SYNC when they were visiting Florida once. "We found out they had gone out to eat but when we found out which restaurant, the waiter said we had just missed them," she explains. "We went to another store and just missed them again, but by then we had to hurry or we would miss the concert. That night we found out my mom had gotten us backstage passes but didn't tell us—we were so happy, Danielle started to cry and I started screaming. I had my pass signed by the whole group."

Jessica Vasquez of Holly Springs, North Carolina, observes, "'N SYNC are really talented and their voices are so beautiful. They really seem to be down-to-earth and all for their fans. They let you see that they are just normal people." Krystal Mosby of Wilmington, California, is not shy about her feelings for 'N SYNC: "I would do anything to meet my babies!" she declares. "I would camp out on the streets for a week! I would swim across a shark-

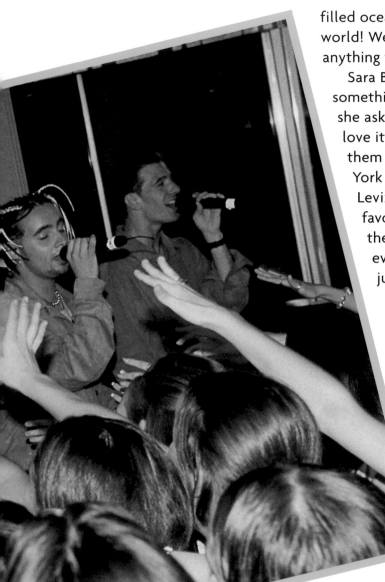

filled ocean. I would climb mountains. I would walk around the world! Well, I am exaggerating now, but I would do just about anything to meet these guys!"

Sara Boothe of Minneapolis, Minnesota, wonders if she did something weird for love of 'N SYNC. "Does a tattoo count?" she asks. "I have their name logo in block letters down my hip. I love it! I live in Minneapolis, but I have gone on trips to see them in Chicago and in Fargo, North Dakota, and I was in New York City for the release of *No Strings Attached*." Melissa Levix of Boca Raton, Florida, admits, "I honestly don't have a favorite, but my favorite thing about all of them is the way they fit together and how much they play off each other. If even one of the guys was missing from the group, they just wouldn't be the same."

Jen Ference from Calgary, Alberta, Canada, says, "When 'N SYNC came to Calgary, we spotted Joey's brother Steve and offered him a ride to Wal-Mart to buy his Christmas gifts and he accepted. He gave us backstage passes—even my dad got one! I got to meet 'N SYNC backstage in Edmonton, Canada, and they were really tired, but they were so incredibly nice to me and all of the other fans around. I loved every second of it, and wish I could relive the whole thing over and over and over. . . I would do anything to meet them all again, except this time with my friends. I would even cut the grass in a football field with nail clippers to see them for two minutes!"

Tiffany Jenkins of Topeka, Kansas, notes, "I don't think I would do anything crazy to meet them. If I knew I was going to have a chance, I'd probably just be myself. I mean, the last thing they'd want to do is hang out with a girl who licked someone's toes or streaked butt naked in front of an old people's home or something like that. It's like, 'Hi, I'm Tiffany and I ate worms to meet you guys, can I get a kiss good-bye?' Yeah, right."

Nikki King of Warwick, Rhode Island, observes, "I am one of the older 'N SYNC fans, so I don't really have a fave member—I like them all. They all seem down-to-earth and they stand up for what they believe in. How many bands would do what they did, take their manager to court and fight for themselves when everyone was saying they were going to lose. They proved all the nonbelievers wrong." Jennie Gagnon of Chicopee, Massachusetts, explains, "My favorite thing about 'N SYNC is their ability to touch so many fans around the world at once. They create the biggest impact on me with just a simple sentence. I feel shivers down my spine just thinking of them. They are truly five in a million!"

Raise your hands if you want to take these guys home for the weekend! Band meets hands at the Double or Nothing Rock the Towers party, World Trade Center, New York City.

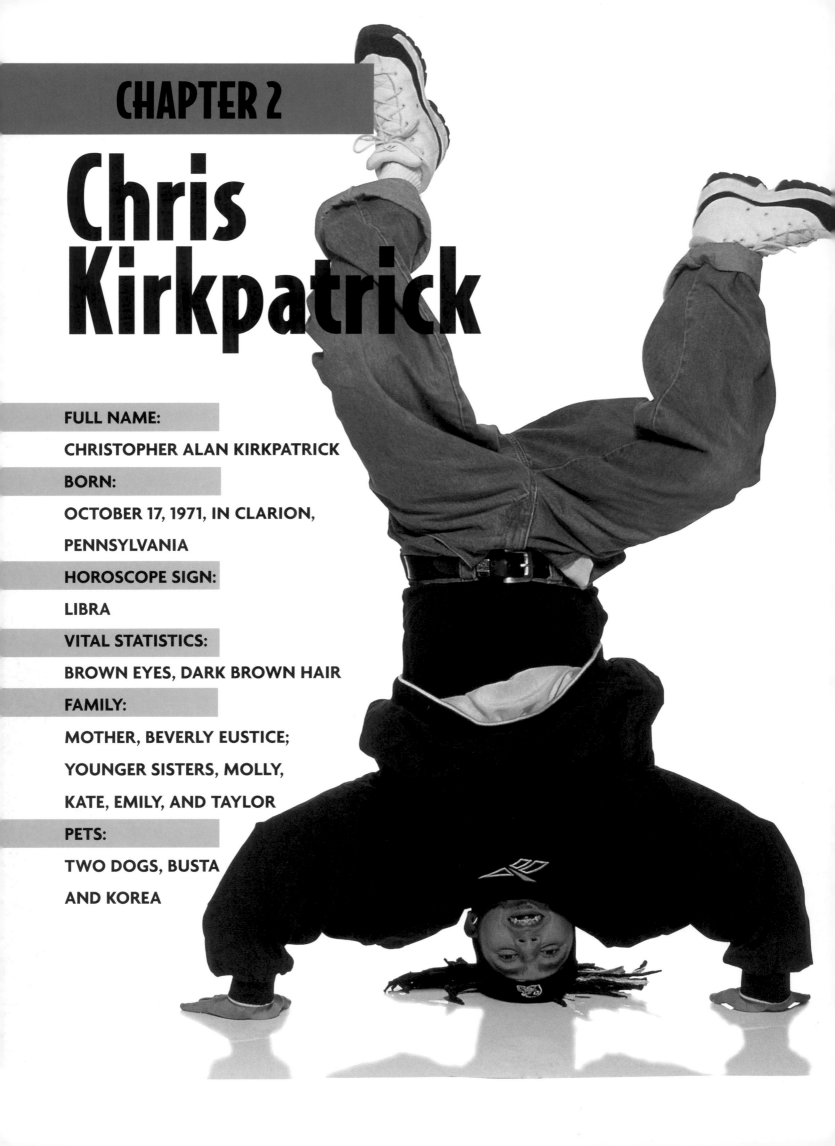

CHAPTER 2
Chris Kirkpatrick

FULL NAME:

CHRISTOPHER ALAN KIRKPATRICK

BORN:

OCTOBER 17, 1971, IN CLARION,

PENNSYLVANIA

HOROSCOPE SIGN:

LIBRA

VITAL STATISTICS:

BROWN EYES, DARK BROWN HAIR

FAMILY:

MOTHER, BEVERLY EUSTICE;

YOUNGER SISTERS, MOLLY,

KATE, EMILY, AND TAYLOR

PETS:

TWO DOGS, BUSTA

AND KOREA

It used to be that even people who didn't really know about 'N SYNC knew something about Chris: "the one with the hair," "the guy with the dreads," "that guy with the freaky hair." Chris's hair was getting to be his trademark, but along with a new record label and a new CD, Chris is sporting a brand-new look that is less radical, more flattering. Perhaps it signals that Chris is becoming more comfortable with himself, so he doesn't need to hide behind an image. Or maybe he was just getting sick of all the time and trouble it took to maintain The Hair. On an AOL chat in January 2000, Chris was asked why he got rid of his dreads. They were annoying, he explained. "It seemed so easy to flow them up into a ponytail, but when I took a shower I had to wash each one," he said. "It took like eight hours to get them rebraided."

Chris is kicking off the new millennium by developing a music production–apparel line called FuMan Skeeto, which will be available online at www.fumanskeeto.com in the very near future. In addition to the apparel line, FuMan Skeeto is promoting and producing work by Canadian singer-songwriter Ron Irazarry, who may open for 'N SYNC during segments of their North American tour.

Opposite: Chris would stand on his head to please his fans!

Right: Chris's dread-less 'do got rave reviews—here he shows off his fashionable new look at the 1999 Billboard Awards.

Above: Was that really your favorite 'N SYNC guy you were chatting to online last night, or was it just a cheap imitation? They'll never tell!

Opposite: Chris in an unusually pensive pose.

Chris's reputation for being a little strange at times is reinforced by the story behind FuMan Skeeto's name. It was in the wee hours of the morning, and one of his braids had been cut off. The fallen braid landed by a big, dead mosquito. "It looked like it had a Fu Manchu mustache," Chris told *Rolling Stone*, "so I called it a FuMan Skeeto."

Far from the rich lifestyle some fans imagine, Chris and the others spend a lot of time living in very unglamorous tour buses when they are on the road. Life on tour can be stressful but it's not all hard work, as Chris explained to *Disney Adventures* magazine. "We play a lot of football and basketball and Mario Golf on the Nintendo. I'm a video-game junkie," he joked. They don't always eat healthy meals when they are touring,

either. Chris confessed to *Teen* magazine, "We all have strange eating habits on the road—we're on the bus for so long, there's nothing to eat but weird food. We eat a lot of fast food, a lot of McDonald's."

Chris's fans explain what they like best about him. Jaime Fletcher of Lawrenceville, New Jersey, says, "My favorite 'N SYNC member would have to be Chris . . . just the way that he acts so crazy all the time, and tries to be at the center of attention. I love it!" Sharon Bailey of El Monte, California, agrees: "I must say that I love them all as a group, but Chris and JC stand out the most. Chris—I love his sense of humor and his style. With JC, I think it's his laugh and his voice." Michelle Lesener of Trail Creek, Indiana, says, "My favorite thing about Chris was actually his dreads because they were so different. Now it has to be his funny humor, with all the wacky yet cute things he does."

Opposite: Here's Chris in 1999 performing at the Thomas and Mach Center in Las Vegas in support of 'N SYNC's self-titled album.

Right: Looking at the world through rose-colored glasses: Chris is ready for anything at the 1999 MTV Music Awards in New York City.

How Well Do You Know Cool, Crazy Chris?

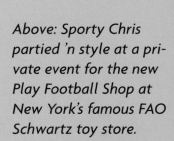

1. When Chris was still in junior high, he got the lead in a high school production of which musical?
a. *Bye Bye Birdie*
b. *Oliver!*
c. *Grease*
d. *West Side Story*

2. What sport does Chris say he doesn't like?
a. Scuba diving
b. Football
c. In-line skating
d. Golf

3. What made Chris fear he was going to have to quit the group?
a. Measles
b. Glasses
c. Braces
d. Stage fright

4. What is Chris's favorite possession?
a. A bear called Shorty
b. One of his dreads that he had bronzed
c. A vintage Harley-Davidson
d. A Bruce Lee autograph

5. Chris's new line of clothing was named after Fu Manchu and what bug?
a. Fly
b. Mosquito
c. Beetle
d. Spider

6. Chris once sang in a fifties-style group called the Hollywood High Tones, performing at Universal Studios in Florida. What was his name in the group?
a. Kookie
b. The Rebel
c. Spike
d. Hot Rod Hank

7. Chris has said that he cut his dreads because it took too long to take care of them. How long did it take to wash them?
a. 3 hours
b. 1 hour
c. 20 minutes
d. 45 minutes

8. Chris says he has one phobia. What is it?
a. Arachnophobia (fear of spiders)
b. Claustrophobia (fear of confined or enclosed spaces)
c. Acrophobia (fear of high places)
d. Agoraphobia (fear of open or public places)

9. What is the focal point of Chris's house?
a. A pool in the middle of the house with a waterfall and a Jacuzzi
b. A log cabin–style living room with massive stone fireplace
c. A large recording studio and movie screening room
d. A wall-size mural painted with likenesses of each 'N SYNC member

10. Chris's mom, Beverly, tells about a doll she once made for Chris out of leftover pieces of bedsheets. What did Chris call that doll?
a. Lefty
b. Joey
c. Mr. Sheet
d. Barney

Above: Sporty Chris partied 'n style at a private event for the new Play Football Shop at New York's famous FAO Schwartz toy store.

Opposite: Wonder if this leopard wishes it could change its spots as often as Chris changes his hair?

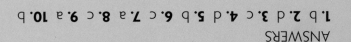

ANSWERS
1. b **2.** d **3.** c **4.** d **5.** b **6.** c **7.** a **8.** c **9.** a **10.** b

Above: Flashing his pearly whites and showing the excellent job braces can do, Chris was looking perky at the 1999 Billboard Music Awards in Las Vegas, Nevada.

Opposite: Chris gazes soulfully out of those big brown eyes (even class clowns have their serious moments!).

CHAPTER 3
JC Chasez

FULL NAME:

JOSHUA SCOTT

CHASEZ

(PRONOUNCED SHA-ZAY)

BORN:

AUGUST 8, 1976, IN BOWIE,

MARYLAND

(NEAR WASHINGTON, D.C.)

HOROSCOPE SIGN:

LEO

VITAL STATISTICS:

BLUE EYES, DARK BROWN HAIR

FAMILY:

PARENTS, ROY AND KAREN CHASEZ;

YOUNGER SISTER, HEATHER; YOUNGER

BROTHER, TYLER

PETS:

A CAT, GRENDAL

JC Chasez is an enigma. Some people describe him as energetic and sensitive, while others call him a perfectionist, serious, sexy, gifted, a deep thinker, quiet and shy, or "Mr. Sleepy." Are they all talking about the same guy? In *'N SYNC's Official Book*, JC describes himself as a workaholic, explaining, "Once I get into something I dive into it with both feet." But he may need a little nudge first. When JC was young, for example, it seemed that everyone else had more confidence in his talent than he did himself. His parents and his dance instructor urged him to take part in a talent competition, yet not until a friend dared him did he finally agree to go on stage. That competition proved to be a turning point in his career, since it indirectly led to his successful audition for the Mickey Mouse Club, where he later met future 'N SYNCer Justin Timberlake.

Although JC's musical and performing skills are indisputable, his interests lie as much behind the scenes as on stage. Being part of a world-famous pop group might seem to be enough for anybody, but not JC. He plays piano and guitar, and brings a keyboard with him on tour. He has written songs for 'N SYNC, including four songs on *No Strings Attached*, and has written songs and done production work for other groups, including Wild Orchid, Blaque, and Boyz and Girlz United; sometimes he even sings backup for them. As JC explained on an AOL chat, "We try to be supportive of up-and-coming people, because we know what it's like to be hungry and want to go out there and be in front of those audiences."

Opposite: JC shows off the moves that make him such an awesome dancer!

Right: JC loses it at the Blockbuster Entertainment Awards in Los Angeles in 1999.

JC's fans have plenty to say about what makes him so special. Kristina Murray of Hibbing, Minnesota, declares, "My favorite 'N SYNC member is JC Chasez. . . . I kind of grew up watching him when he was on the Mickey Mouse Club. Also, I think he has one of the most amazing voices I have heard on the airwaves in a very long time. He sings with such passion that it gives me chills to listen to him." Tracey Plouffe of Saco, Montana, says, "My favorite thing about

Opposite: When asked about nicknames the guys have for each other in an AOL chat, JC said, "As if my name isn't short enough, they call me 'C'!"

Above: Who could resist such a captivating smile? JC's fans think he's the greatest, whether he's elegantly attired or just wearing jeans.

JC is the fact that he is a talented song-writer and producer. He never ceases to amaze me with his talent and hard work—I admire him so much!"

Jaime Fletcher of Lawrenceville, New Jersey, had a "close encounter" with JC last summer: "I got to hang out with JC at their hotel last summer in Philly. He was incredibly sweet and we talked a lot about music, how the band got together, what inspires him and so on, and what it's like to go on tour." Kelly Ryan of Erie, Pennsylvania, says, "My favorite thing about JC is that he is himself. He doesn't try to act like someone he's not just so people will like him. I also love how passionate he is about the music—he's about being heard, and not being seen."

Left: Wonder if these guys ever get used to seeing their faces on magazine covers? JC poses with a cover shot of JC and four other guys at Teen People's first anniversary party in 1999.

Opposite: JC Chasez loves the performing part of his career; here he pours his energy into a performance at the Thomas & Mach Center in 1999.

How Well Do You Know Jumpin', Jivin' JC ?

Opposite: JC's fans have no doubt about his power to tame a wild beast, and what they wouldn't give to trade places with this leopard!

Above: Chill! JC looks cool and calm at the Blockbuster Entertainment Awards in 1999.

1. JC always wears a necklace with what animal on it?
a. A lion
b. A dolphin
c. A horse
d. A koala bear

2. How many songs did JC write on the *No Strings Attached* album?
a. Three
b. None
c. One
d. Four

3. In a BBC Online interview, the guys were asked what they do when they are just too tired and don't want to get out of bed in the morning. Justin said, "We think of all the children out there," but JC cut in with a quick reply. What was it?
a. "We think of what our fans would do to us if we didn't show up."
b. "We throw a glass of cold water on anyone too lazy to get out of bed."
c. "We just think of our whole audience in underwear."
d. "We take pictures of whoever is still snoring in bed and blackmail them later."

4. Joey collects Superman memorabilia. What does JC collect?
a. Beanie Babies
b. *Star Wars* collectibles
c. Hard Rock Cafe menus
d. Autographs of celebrities he has met

5. In the video of "I Drive Myself Crazy," JC's pajamas sport pictures of what?
a. Mickey Mouse and Donald Duck
b. Road Runner and Wile E. Coyote
c. The Spice Girls
d. Aliens and yellow elephants

6. What was the name of the character JC played on the new Mickey Mouse Club's weekly drama "Emerald Cove"?
a. Richie Cunningham
b. Clarence "Wipeout" Adams
c. Bobby Brady
d. Frankie "The Flash" Faulkner

7. JC admits to a fear of what?
a. Sharks
b. Spiders
c. Needles
d. Dentist's drills

8. JC did some production work on which girl group's new album?
a. Dixie Chicks
b. Wild Orchid
c. Indigo Girls
d. The Go-Go's

9. In the March 30, 2000, issue of *Rolling Stone* magazine, JC talks about the video for "Bye Bye Bye," especially the scene where the guys are running from Guess? model Kim Smith. JC says that in the video they are running from her because they are:
a. Afraid of her
b. Late for a concert
c. Stupid
d. Following a script

10. Christina Aguilera recalls in *Rolling Stone* that during Mickey Mouse Club days, she once got very mad at the young JC when he told her to do what?
a. "Go fly a kite."
b. "Go bother somebody else."
c. "Go put some makeup on."
d. "Go play with your Barbie dolls."

ANSWERS
1. a **2.** d **3.** c **4.** c **5.** d **6.** d **7.** c **8.** b **9.** c **10.** d

Above: Ericka Heinbokel, a major fan of JC's from Cincinnati, Ohio, says, "JC is my dream guy. He's hypnotizing. His amazing voice and his chiseled good looks make him heaven sent with no strings attached!"

Opposite: With his sharp fashion sense and classic good looks, JC could easily pursue a career as a model. But this talented guy would rather write and produce songs in his spare time!

CHAPTER 4
Driving the Girls Crazy

Above: Lance is all wrapped up in Britney Spears, but Joey's thoughts seem far away!

Right: Bringin 'Da Noise: 'N SYNC performing in New York City in 1999.

Above: They Got It: 'N SYNC exercising their right to harmonize in 1997 in Munich, Germany.

Opposite: Joey singin' backup vocals to an 'N SYNC tune in New York.

No one knows a band like their fans do, except maybe the families of the band members. But even the most doting mother would not show her affection in the extreme ways that fans sometimes do. Take, for instance, the infamous episode of the French toast. It all started in March 2000 when 'N SYNC visited the wild New York radio station Z100, where the band members had breakfast with some contest winners. A member of the radio staff was the first to notice that one of the band members—first said to be Justin, later confirmed to be Lance—

had left an uneaten
piece of French toast
on his plate.

As a joke, some-
one bid a dollar or
so on the stale
food. Word of the bid-
ding spread like wildfire, with the
high bidder paying $1,025 for the left-
overs. Although the winner was reported-
ly a college student whose mother was
less than pleased with her spendthrift
ways, www.nsyncstudio.com later report-
ed that the girl did receive a pair of free

concert tickets to help justify the price she paid. The clear winners in this exchange were the 'N SYNC charities that will split the profits from this unorthodox auction.

'N SYNC fans did not appear too surprised when this episode caused a media frenzy. A quick look at eBay reveals that fans will spend good money on everything from buttons that have been torn off clothes, to smelly old shoes, to posters ripped out of magazines. Is there a limit to what fans will do for 'N SYNC? Fan Jaime Fletcher of Lawrenceville, New Jersey, writes, "I would probably wait thousands of hours in line at an auto-

Above: Melissa Joan Hart looks completely bewitched by JC's enchanting smile.

Center: Joey's fans think he's a super man, as they mingle at FAO Schwartz's Play Football Shop.

graph table, even though I know that I'll only get to say 'hi' and 'bye.'" Kristina Murray of Hibbing, Minnesota, elaborates, "I would be willing to go club-hopping—with friends—to find out where they are partying, losing money on the cover charges at each club until we found them." Kristina does have limits, though. "I try not to do anything too outlandish," she stresses. "I wouldn't want them to remember me as the girl who tried to ride on the luggage carousel at the airport!"

Above: Joey lives up to his reputation as a lady's man with actress Jennifer Tilly.

Back in the day: 'N SYNC as they were in 1997. (L–R) JC Chasez, Joey Fatone, Chris Kirkpatrick, Justin Timberlake, and Lance Bass.

Giving Their All: 'N SYNC Loves Charities

The guys in 'N SYNC have their hearts in the right places. They may be bringing in some of the biggest bucks in the music industry, but they haven't forgotten that there are plenty of good causes struggling for money. Even with schedules so tight they barely have time to breathe sometimes, all five guys have made time to support charities that are important to them.

Of course, it isn't all hard work. They were pretty excited to be invited to VH1's Concert of the Century at the White House, along with such music legends as Eric Clapton, Garth Brooks, Gloria Estefan, and Sheryl Crow. The event was held to raise awareness about the "Save the Music" campaign, encouraging schools to keep their music programs even when budgets get tight. The cause is very close to the hearts of all the 'N SYNC members, especially Justin, who has started his own foundation supporting music in schools. While fame is nothing new to the guys, this event had them starry-eyed. They rubbed shoulders with Gwyneth Paltrow, Joey chatted with Lenny Kravitz, and Lance got to meet his favorite musician, Garth Brooks. Just being there was a buzz, as Justin summed up in *J-14* magazine, "Meeting and performing for the President is a huge honor," he raved, adding that he could hardly believe he was really there.

In August 1999, 'N SYNC organized a charity basketball game and took to the courts to raise money for Arnold Palmer's Hospital for Children and Women, based in Orlando, Florida, and the Atlanta Hawks Foundation. Called "Challenge for the Children," the event brought together a room full of celebrities at the campus of Georgia State University in Atlanta. After a kick-off at Planet Hollywood, things got serious (sort of). The guys played hard for a good cause, and everyone had plenty of fun. The coaches included the L.A. Lakers' Kobe Bryant, Antwan Jamison of the Golden State Warriors, Reggie Miller of the Indiana Pacers, and Dennis Scott of the Vancouver Grizzlies. The teams boasted an all-star lineup, including JC, Chris, and Lance playing for The Daze with teammates Usher, Jon Seda, and 'N SYNC manager Johnny Wright, while Justin and Joey's team, The Knights, included Brian McKnight, Tyrese, and Eric Williams and Terrell Phillips of Blackstreet. The game was such a success that 'N SYNC is organizing a replay of this event in summer 2000.

The 'N SYNC gang also got together in November 1999 for the Team Harmony VI event to promote diversity, tolerance, and acceptance. Held at Boston's FleetCenter, the event united students from Massachusetts, New Hampshire, Rhode Island, Maine, and

New York in an interactive rally to combat all kinds of discrimination, racism, and hatred. Other celebrities there to support the cause with 'N SYNC included the band No Authority, gymnast Dominique Dawes, and Boston Red Sox player Mo Vaughn.

Justin is making a name for himself as a philanthropist, after creating the Justin Timberlake Foundation to help make more funds available for quality music programs in public schools. In October 1999, Justin announced that his foundation would partner with the Giving Back Fund, a national nonprofit organization that helps professional athletes, entertainers, and other celebrities channel some of their wealth to worthy causes by establishing charitable foundations. First Lady Hillary Clinton invited Justin to Washington, D.C., to join in a White House conference on philanthropy; while in Washington, Justin also spoke about his cause to students at some of the capital's elementary schools.

And Justin's not the only 'N SYNC name in the news. In March 2000 Chris Kirkpatrick was made an official spokesperson for the national organization ChildWatch, whose goal is to locate missing children.

Another way the group makes their mark is with children who are sick or needy, by donating many of the items fans throw on the stage during 'N SYNC concerts. (They do keep special favorites, but there really is no way they could keep them all.) Because they know that these souvenirs—many of them cuddly toys—are given with love, they make sure the fans' gifts are appreciated by donating many items to children's hospitals and similar charities. They have also donated their vocal talents on singles such as "Feed the World," on which Sting and other major stars came together to raise money in the fight against hunger. They even joined their so-called archrivals the Backstreet Boys (in real life, they get along fine), calling the combined groups the Bravo All-Stars on the single "Let the Music Heal Your Soul," benefiting a music therapy foundation.

As 'N SYNC reaches the pinnacle of success, each of the members will certainly be dedicating his valuable—and very rare—spare time, as well as his money, to a number of worthy causes.

Doing what they do best: 'N SYNC puts heart and soul into a performance for "Music with a Message: World AIDS Day."

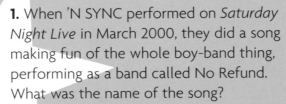

All 'N SYNC, All the Time

1. When 'N SYNC performed on *Saturday Night Live* in March 2000, they did a song making fun of the whole boy-band thing, performing as a band called No Refund. What was the name of the song?
a. "My Salsa Señorita"
b. "Supersize It"
c. "If You Make Seven-Up Yours, Why Can't I Make You Mine?"
d. "I'll Be Your Abercrombie, if You'll Be My Fitch"

2. On MTV's "'N SYNC Live" performance, in March 2000, the whole band agreed on their favorite video of the moment. What video was it? (Hint: The performer's daughter, Zoe, is a big 'N SYNC fan!)
a. Destiny's Child, "Say My Name"
b. Blaque, "Bring It All to Me"
c. Lenny Kravitz, "Fly Away"
d. Moby, "Natural Blues"

3. Which small island nations recently announced that they will be issuing postage stamps featuring 'N SYNC?
a. Trinidad and Tobago
b. Cayman Brac and Little Cayman (sister islands)
c. Tenerife and Lanzarote (Canary Islands)
d. St. Vincent and the Grenadines (Caribbean islands)

4. In 1998, 'N SYNC was the opening act for which performer's tour?
a. Janet Jackson
b. Spice Girls
c. Jennifer Lopez
d. Gloria Estefan

5. In an online interview on an AOL chat in January 2000, JC Chasez discussed how they first got together as a group by singing a capella songs. What was the first song they sang together?
a. "The Lion Sleeps Tonight"
b. "In the Still of the Night"
c. "How Deep Is Your Love"
d. "Here, There, and Everywhere"

6. In the import video for the European single "U Drive Me Crazy," the guys dress up as different groups and pretend to audition for a recording contract. In a memorable scene, they dressed up as Spice Girls, with Justin as Sporty Spice, Lance as Baby Spice, Chris as Scary Spice, JC as Posh Spice, and Joey as Ginger Spice. What other famous band did they pretend to be?
a. The Rolling Stones
b. The Temptations
c. The Jackson 5
d. The Brady Bunch

Below: The guys show their true colors as 'N SYNC performs at the Universal Amphitheatre in California in 1999.

7. Which band member rounds out the 'N SYNC sound with his deep voice?
a. Joey Fatone
b. Chris Kirkpatrick
c. JC Chasez
d. Lance Bass

8. In the early days of 'N SYNC, the group made a guest appearance on ABC's *Sabrina, the Teenage Witch*. What song did they perform on the show?
a. "Crazy for You"
b. "For the Girl Who Has Everything"
c. "Tearin' Up My Heart"
d. "Sailing"

9. Which band member slipped and fell during a European concert, breaking his thumb?
a. Justin Timberlake
b. Lance Bass
c. Joey Fatone
d. Chris Kirkpatrick

10. On the cover of *Rolling Stone* in March 2000, the guys were sprayed, glued, dressed, and decorated with this stuff:
a. Marshmallow fluff
b. Silver glitter
c. Chicken feathers
d. Paintball glops

CHAPTER 5
Justin Timberlake

FULL NAME:

JUSTIN RANDALL TIMBERLAKE

BORN:

JANUARY 31, 1981, IN MEMPHIS, TENNESSEE

HOROSCOPE SIGN:

AQUARIUS

VITAL STATISTICS:

BLUE EYES, BLOND HAIR

FAMILY:

MOTHER AND STEPFATHER,
LYNN AND PAUL HARLESS;
YOUNGER BROTHERS, JONATHAN
AND STEVEN; FATHER AND
STEPMOTHER, RANDY AND
LISA TIMBERLAKE

PETS:

FAMILY DOG,
OZZIE, AND
CAT, ALLEY

Justin Timberlake may be the youngest member of 'N SYNC, but that doesn't make him low man on the totem pole. His career started at a very early age: he appeared on *Star Search* at age eleven and joined the Mickey Mouse Club team when he was only twelve. By the time he joined 'N SYNC, Justin was already a seasoned performer. Still, he may not have anticipated that his musical success would also bring him the label of teen heartthrob. If there was ever any doubt, it's now official—Justin was selected for an issue of *Teen People* magazine entitled, "The 21 Hottest Stars under 21."

Perhaps because of his image as "the cute, curly-haired one," Justin can get a little defensive when the subject of his popularity with young girls comes up. In a *Rolling Stone* interview he stressed, "We don't try to make ourselves do cute, we just are who we are." In particular, Justin seems anxious that the new CD, *No Strings Attached*, is not lumped into the "boy band" genre. "There's a little more edge to this album," he told *Rolling Stone*, "a little more grit." While the sudden fame was a little hard on him, Justin says that his spirituality has helped him through.

Like the others, Justin is enjoying working with "no strings" and exploring new aspects of his career. As he explained in an AOL chat, "We really feel like we are coming into our own and that nobody can hold us back from really creating what we want to for our careers." In March 2000 he appeared in an ABC-TV movie, *Model Behavior*, playing the part

Left: Justin drives himself crazy, as he proves in this shot taken in 1998 in Los Angeles.

Right: Superfan Amanda Smith of Cincinnati, Ohio, says: "I like Justin's style. He's very sporty, yet clean-cut. I like the way he carries himself; he has a lot of confidence." That says it all!

of a teenage supermodel and getting his first on-screen kiss. Justin told *People* magazine, "It wasn't Shakespeare," but added that he didn't care what critics said about his acting since he was only doing it for fun.

Justin takes his charity work very seriously, though. His efforts to promote music education programs in schools through the Justin Timberlake Foundation and the Giving It Back Fund have been recognized by First Lady Hillary Clinton, who invited Justin to Washington, D.C., to help promote his cause.

Krystal Londono from Albrightsville, Pennsylvania, is a big fan of Justin's. "I think my favorite thing about Justin is that he has such a beautiful voice and that he is such a great dancer! I went backstage at one of their concerts and I was the only one not crying. Justin came up and asked me my name, then started screaming, 'Oh my god, there's Krystal!' It was so cute!" Christine Sinclair says, "My favorite thing about Justin is that he is extremely funny. He is the greatest guy in the world!"

Krystal Mosby of Wilmington, California, says, "My favorite guy is Justin. What I love about him is that he is so real. He doesn't try to be the ideal famous person—he is who he is, and I love him for that. He seems like someone I would know, because he is so down-to-earth. Plus he is drop-dead gorgeous!" Kristine Leon of Kearny, New Jersey, adds, "My favorite thing about Justin is that he is a normal teenager—he plays basketball, video games, does regular teenage stuff. He just has a way better job than most teenagers!"

Left: Many girls would agree that God must've spent a little more time on Justin, performing here at the Nassau Coliseum in New York in March 1999.

Opposite: The face that launched a thousand fans—Justin proves he's not just a kid anymore.

Above: Who says girls don't make passes at guys who wear glasses? Heartbreaker Justin meets the press at the twenty-seventh Annual American Music Awards in Los Angeles, 2000.

Right: It's no good—you can run, Justin, but you can't hide the hair and get away with it!

1. In an AOL-Live interview in March 2000, what did Justin say was his favorite movie?
a. *The Sixth Sense*
b. *E.T.*
c. *Ferris Bueller's Day Off*
d. *Scream*

2. When the group is on the road, what dessert does Justin miss most?
a. His mom's pecan pie
b. His Aunt Amy's strawberry shortcake
c. His mom's double chocolate cake
d. His grandmother's peach cobbler

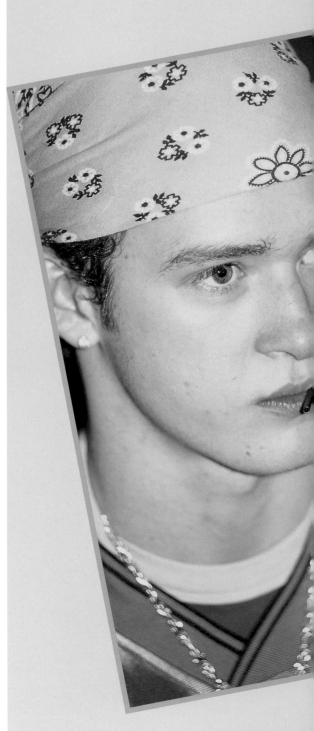

How Well Do You Know Bouncing, Blue-eyed Justin?

3. What is the name of the charitable organization Justin founded to help put music back into schools?
a. The Justin Timberlake Foundation
b. The Music for Kids Organization
c. The School Sounds Foundation
d. The Music Preservation Foundation

4. What men's fragrance does Justin like to wear?
a. Tommy Hilfiger
b. Abercrombie & Fitch "Woods"
c. Davidoff "Cool Water"
d. Hugo "Boss"

5. Justin's aunt and uncle introduced him to a Cincinnati-based brand of ice cream that he now loves. He hasn't named a favorite flavor but admits he likes the coffee ice cream. Who makes this ice cream?
a. Graeter's
b. Baskin Robbins
c. Carvel's
d. Edy's

6. Justin says meeting this sports celebrity really meant a lot to him. Who was he?
a. Tiger Woods
b. Walter Payton
c. Andre Agassi
d. Michael Jordan

7. Justin's mom, Lynn Harless, manages the girl group Innosense. What's the name of her management company?
a. Synchronicity
b. Just-In Time Entertainment
c. In-Tune With Timberlake, Inc.
d. Mother Knows Best, Ltd.

8. What is Justin's favorite sport?
a. Football
b. Soccer
c. Basketball
d. Tennis

9. What is Justin's latest new car?
a. A classic red '57 Chevy
b. A metallic gold Ford Expedition
c. A baby-blue Ferrari convertible
d. A purple-blue BMW M roadster

10. In 'N SYNC's official book, what does Justin's mom remember was his favorite toy?
a. A plush toy chimpanzee
b. Different toy guitars
c. A ten-speed bike
d. A raggedy toy tiger

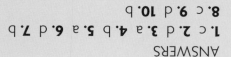

ANSWERS
1. c 2. d 3. a 4. b 5. a 6. d 7. b
8. c 9. d 10. b

Above: Justin gives a whole new meaning to wet T-shirt contests as he cools off in Los Angeles, 1998.

Opposite: Pierced to perfection: Justin Randall Timberlake in 1998.

CHAPTER 6
Lance Bass

FULL NAME:

JAMES LANCE BASS

BORN:

MAY 4, 1979, IN CLINTON, MISSISSIPPI

HOROSCOPE SIGN:

TAURUS

VITAL STATISTICS:

GREEN EYES, BLOND HAIR

FAMILY:

PARENTS, DIANE AND JIM BASS; OLDER SISTER, STACY

PETS:

NONE

Lance may have been the last to join 'N SYNC, but he has been on equal footing with the others from the start. He has a reputation for being somewhat laid back and shy, which seems to conflict with other descriptions of him as hardworking and businesslike. No one disputes the friendliness and courtesy that, back in his school days, earned him the title "Friendliest Student," or the charm that led *Teen People* magazine to refer to him as a "Southern gentleman." Parents can relax when their daughters follow Lance's example. He doesn't say that he and the other guys in the group are perfect, but as he explained to *Rolling Stone*, "We do have a responsibility to be morally correct."

You might think the guys in 'N SYNC would be used to the world of celebrities by now, but when they were invited to perform their Oscar-nominated song, "Music of My Heart," at the Academy Awards ceremony in March 2000, Lance was anything but cool. After revealing to *USA Today* that they would be wearing Dolce & Gabbana tuxedos to the event, Lance confessed, "I really want to meet Julia Roberts; she's been one of my all-time favorite actresses. And I love Sandra Bullock. I'm a huge movie buff. I'm like a little kid in a candy store."

Lance had his own brush with nonmusical fame when he made a guest appearance on the WB-TV series *7th Heaven* in January 2000, a performance highlighted by a much-publicized kiss with the show's costar Beverley Mitchell. On an AOL chat, Lance was asked about that kiss. "She's a great kisser, but it was an acting

Opposite: There are no strings on Lance—he must have just heard the numbers for NSA's first week of sales!

Right: Lance may look dreamy but he's also a level-headed businessman with his own company.

Above: Lance may seem kind of quiet and shy, but his fans know he also has a wild side!

Opposite: Lance likes the movie Grease, and with his leather look here he could be hoping for a remake.

kiss," he explained. "It's weird when there's fifty people watching you."

Lance does not need to look to television for a second career; he already has one. Besides his pretty much full-time job as a member of 'N SYNC, Lance also operates a management company called Free Lance Entertainment. His mother and sister help run the company, which manages the careers of such country performers as Meredith Edwards and Jack Defeo.

Lance is bothered that many people seem to make unfair judgments about the group. He told *J-14* magazine for a special 'N SYNC edition, "People's misconcep-

How Well Do You Know Lucky, Laid-Back Lance?

1. Lance says that his favorite movie of 1999 was *The Sixth Sense*. What movie did he see on St. Patrick's Day, 2000? (Hint: It scared him a lot!)
a. *Mission to Mars*
b. *Final Destination*
c. *Reindeer Games*
d. *Scream 3*

2. While rehearsing for a *Saturday Night Live* performance in March 2000, Lance suffered an injury. What was it?
a. A bloody nose
b. A dislocated shoulder
c. A sprained ankle
d. A broken toe

3. As if being in an extremely successful pop group was not enough, Lance helps develop country music artists on the side. What is the name of his recording and management company?
a. Bass Notes, Inc.
b. Synchronicity Corporation
c. Lanston Links, Inc.
d. Free Lance Management

4. Lance recently shared his first screen kiss on the TV show *7th Heaven*. What is the name of the character played by the girl he kissed?
a. Lucy Camden
b. Kelly Martin
c. Alice Kramden
d. Jennifer Love Hewitt

5. An appliance belonging to Lance—one he says he can't live without—was stolen. What was it?
a. His electric shaver
b. His Discman
c. His cell phone
d. His pager

6. What has Lance described as his most embarrassing moment?
a. Having his pants fall down on stage
b. Fighting a bull in Mexico
c. Saying Michael Jackson was a hero of his, when he meant Michael Jordan
d. Seeing one of his former teachers screaming in the audience at a concert

7. Lance has a tattoo of tiny flames on what part of his body?
a. His ankle
b. His shoulder blade
c. His big toe
d. His wrist

8. At one time Lance wanted to work for which organization?
a. MTV
b. Microsoft
c. NASA
d. The Dallas Cowboys

9. In a *Teen* magazine article in April 2000, a psychic predicted Lance would one day have two sons. Lance indicated that if so, he would give them interesting names. What name did he say he liked?
a. Alonzo
b. River
c. Xander
d. Wolf

10. Lance has said that he would like to design one of these someday:
a. A roller coaster
b. A golf course
c. A concept car
d. A CD cover

tions are the biggest problem we have," noting that many assumed they made music only for ten-year-olds. "We make music for everybody, which everybody's finally realizing now." Looking to the future. Lance hopes that in twenty years the group will still be together with lots of tours and albums behind them. He predicted to *J-14*, "I see us doing individual stuff, too. Solo albums. Movies. We want to do every aspect of the business."

Fans have no complaints where Lance is concerned. Estee Ratliff of Philadelphia says, "My favorite 'N SYNC member is Lance because he seems laid back and down-to-earth," adding that she would drive all night if she had a chance to meet them.

Korie Cherry, a fan from Cincinnati, Ohio, was first attracted to Lance because of his morals and values as well as his family relationships. "My mom has always told me that you can tell how a man will treat you by the way he treats his mother," she explains. "My mom is my best friend so it means something that Lance treats his mom with so much respect."

Lance points to a lucky fan at a 1999 concert in Long Island, New York.

Above: It's hard being a world-class celebrity! Lance unwinds and soaks up some rays in Crete, 1998.

Opposite: "Look into my eyes," says Lance. This southern gentleman has green eyes that hypnotize.

CHAPTER 7

Diamonds Are a Band's Best Friend

Above: Double the pleasure, double the fun with the hottest group on ten legs, pictured here in New York City, 1999.

Right: Always up for helping a good cause, 'N SYNC gave an energetic performance at the 1999 World AIDS Day concert at the Beacon Theater in New York City.

They just want some respect, and by now they've earned it. 'N SYNC has skyrocketed to the top of the pops, capturing many coveted awards along the way, with many more sure to follow. Gold records, platinum records, and then in early 2000 'N SYNC's 1998 self-titled debut album garnered the Recording Industry Association of America's Diamond Award when the CD hit ten million in sales. As impressive as this sounds, sales of the new CD No Strings Attached, certified seven times platinum for shipping 7 million copies in only five weeks, have already blown these numbers out of the water.

They have scooped up Billboard Music Video Awards, including Best Clip of the Year and Best New Artist of the Year, as well as Best New Artist at the American Music Awards, Favorite Music Artists and CD of the Year from AOL's Entertainment Asylum, two Grammy nominations, and a Nickelodeon award. To kick off 2000, "Music of My Heart," which 'N SYNC recorded with Gloria Estefan for Meryl Streep's *Music of the Heart*, was nominated for an Academy Award for Best Original Song from a Motion Picture Soundtrack. Although the song did not win the award, 'N SYNC was brought in to perform it in front of an all-star audience at the ceremony on March 26, 2000.

Even before the long-anticipated release of the CD *No Strings Attached* (it was delayed when the group switched from RCA Records to Jive Records/Zomba last fall), the single "Bye Bye Bye" hit the radio stations running. Music industry sources noted that in its first week of release, the single was the number-one most-added track at more than two hundred contemporary radio stations, breaking a record set by the Backstreet Boys' single "I Want It That Way." In an unusual

JC, Joey, Chris, Justin, and Lance have a laugh at the 1999 American Music Awards in Los Angeles.

move, the single was only released in Europe prior to the release of *No Strings Attached*, and U.S. stores were banned from selling the single as an import—a tactic that was probably intended to boost anticipation and first-week sales for the CD. The single, "Bye Bye Bye," received some advantageous airplay when 'N SYNC performed it at the American Music Awards show in January 2000. (Some media sources repeatedly confused the CD title *No Strings Attached* with the single title "Bye Bye Bye.")

Whatever the plan was to increase sales of *No Strings Attached*, it obviously worked. Some four million copies of the CD were shipped to record stores just prior to the release date of March 22, 2000, in anticipation of high first-day sales and to cover advance orders. First-day sales were 950,000, once again breaking a record set by the Backstreet Boys, this time for first-day sales of that group's 1999 album, *Millennium*.

No Strings Attached is currently the best-selling album of all time. In the fifth week of sales, it was still number one on *Billboard*'s top 200, and garnered "greatest gains" in one-week sales.

Clearly, 'N SYNC is breaking any records that stand in the way. A word to the presenters of the major music awards: remember those names—Justin, JC, Chris, Lance, and Joey will be engraved on plaques and statuettes for some time to come.

Left: Justin makes the girls go crazy for him with his silky voice and boyish good looks.

Opposite: "Superman" and his cape: Joey takes a spin onstage at the Thomas & Mach Center.

Too close for comfort? 'N SYNC back in 1997.

'N SYNC's Music and Media Catalogue

'N SYNC

1. Tearin' Up My Heart
2. I Just Wanna Be With You
3. Here We Go
4. For the Girl Who Has Everything
5. God Must Have Spent a Little More Time on You
6. You Got It
7. I Need Love
8. I Want You Back
9. Everything I Own
10. I Drive Myself Crazy
11. Crazy for You
12. Sailing
13. Giddy Up

Home For Christmas

1. Home for Christmas
2. Under My Tree
3. I Never Knew the Meaning of Christmas
4. Merry Christmas, Happy Holidays
5. The Christmas Song
6. I Guess It's Christmas Time
7. All I Want Is You (This Christmas)
8. The First Noel
9. In Love on Christmas
10. It's Christmas
11. O Holy Night
12. Love's in Our Hearts on Christmas Day
13. The Only Gift
14. Kiss Me at Midnight

No Strings Attached

1. Bye Bye Bye
2. It's Gonna Be Me
3. Space Cowboy
4. Just Got Paid
5. It Makes Me Ill
6. This I Promise You
7. No Strings Attached
8. Digital Get Down
9. Bringin' Da Noise
10. That's When I'll Stop Loving You
11. I'll Be Good For You
12. I Thought She Knew

The Winter Album (Import CD, Germany)

1. U Drive Me Crazy (Radio Edit)
2. God Must Have Spent a Little More Time on You
3. Thinking of You (I Drive Myself Crazy)
4. Everything I Own
5. I Just Wanna Be With You
6. Kiss Me at Midnight
7. Merry Christmas, Happy Holidays
8. All I Want Is You (This Christmas)
9. Under My Tree
10. Love's in Our Hearts on Christmas Day
11. In Love on Christmas
12. The First Noel

'N SYNC (Self-titled import CD), Australia; includes bonus tracks

1. Tearin' Up My Heart
2. I Just Wanna Be With You
3. Here We Go
4. For the Girl Who Has Everything
5. God Must Have Spent a Little More Time On You
6. You Got It
7. I Need Love
8. I Want You Back
9. Everything I Own
10. I Drive Myself Crazy
11. Crazy For You
12. Sailing
13. Giddy Up
14. Sailing (Live)
15. More Than a Feeling
16. Sundreams
17. Tearin' Up My Heart (Phat Dub)
18. I Want You Back (Back Beat Radio Edit)

Singles

I Want You Back
Tearin' Up My Heart
Tearin' Up My Heart (Remix; Europe)
Here We Go (Europe)
God Must Have Spent a Little More Time on You

For the Girl Who Has Everything
U Drive Me Crazy (Europe)
Together Again (Europe)
I Want You Back (Europe)
Thinking of You (Europe)
Merry Christmas, Happy Holidays
Bye Bye Bye

Music Videos
"I Want You Back" (U.S.)
"I Want You Back" (Europe)
"Tearin' Up My Heart"
"Here We Go"
"Merry Christmas, Happy Holidays"
"God Must Have Spent a Little More
    Time on You"
"For the Girl Who Has Everything"
"U Drive Me Crazy"
"I Drive Myself Crazy"
"Music of My Heart"
"Bye Bye Bye"

Other Import CDs and CD Singles
Import, Australia
"I Want You Back"
"Tearin' Up My Heart" (5-inch CD single)

Import, Austria
"God Must Have Spent a Little More
    Time on You" (5-inch CD single)

Import, Germany
"U Drive Me Crazy" (5-inch CD single)

Import, United Kingdom
"Double Whammy"
"For The Girl Who Has Everything"
    (5-inch CD single; also available as
    German import)
"I Want You Back, Part 2"
"Thinking of You" (5-inch CD single; also
    available as German import)
"Together Again" (5-inch CD single)

Other CDs
Puzzles in Motion (CD-Rom Game, 1999)
All Talk (Import, U.K.)
Maximum 'N SYNC, Unauthorised
    (Import, U.K.)

'N SYNC: Popview Interview (Import, U.K.)
'N SYNC: Star Profile (1999)
'N SYNC: Official Interview CD (1999)
Alabama: Twentieth Century (1999; track
    2: 'N SYNC sings backup on Alabama's
    version of "God Must Have Spent a
    Little More Time on You")
Idols of the Pops 2000 (1999; various
    artists; track 9: 'N SYNC, "God Must
    Have Spent a Little More Time
    On You")
Tarzan soundtrack (1999; track 7: Phil
    Collins and 'N SYNC, "Trashin' the
    Camp")
Music of the Heart soundtrack (1999;
    track 1: "Music of My Heart," 'N SYNC
    and Gloria Estefan). This Diane
    Warren song, nominated for Best
    Song from a Motion Picture
    Soundtrack, was performed by
    'N SYNC at the Academy Awards on
    March 26, 2000.
A Rosie Christmas (1999; Rosie
    O'Donnell and various artists; track 5:
    'N SYNC, "Love's in Our Hearts on
    Christmas Day")

DVDS and Videos
'N the Mix Official Home Video (VHS)
'N the Mix (DVD)
No Strings Attached (DVD)

Test Your CD IQ

See how many of these questions you can answer correctly without checking the liner notes first!

1. On the new CD *No Strings Attached*, Lisa "Left Eye" Lopes from the girl group TLC is featured on one song. Which song is it?
a. "No Strings Attached"
b. "Giddy Up"
c. "Space Cowboy (Yippie-Yi-Yay)"
d. "Home on the Range"

2. What is the longest song on *No Strings Attached*?
a. "I'll Be so Good for You"
b. "Sailing"
c. "Digital Get Down"
d. "That's When I'll Stop Loving You"

3. On their premiere album *'N SYNC*, the entire group was credited as co-writer of which song?
a. "Giddy Up"
b. "I Want You Back"
c. "I Need Love"
d. "Crazy for You"

4. What is the title of the group's Christmas album?
a. *Happy Holidays*
b. *Home for Christmas*
c. *Under My Tree*
d. *It's Christmas*

5. In January 2000, 'N SYNC's self-titled 1998 American debut album reached a plateau of ten million in sales, thereby earning which award from the Recording Industry Association of America (RIAA)?
a. Bronze Award
b. Ruby Award
c. Diamond Award
d. Platinum Award

6. Which of the following is not the name of an 'N SYNC CD (album, single, import)?
a. *Star Sounds*
b. *'N SYNC, The Winter Album*
c. *'N SYNC*
d. *"Bye Bye Bye"*

7. JC Chasez helped write several songs on the *No Strings Attached* CD. Which of the following did he *not* write?
a. "Bringin' Da Noise"
b. "That's When I'll Stop Loving You"
c. "Digital Get Down"
d. "No Strings Attached"

8. The first-day sales for *No Strings Attached* were estimated to be about how much?
a. 525,000
b. 1.3 million
c. 780,000
d. 950,000

9. Which of the following was *not* released as an import single?
a. "U Drive Me Crazy"
b. "You Got It"
c. "Thinking of You"
d. "Tearin' Up My Heart"

10. Who produced "It Makes Me Ill" on the *No Strings Attached* CD?
a. L'il Kim
b. Lenny Kravitz
c. She'kespere
d. Kid Rock

Above: The guys of 'N SYNC love to sing non-album tracks like "Ain't No Stopping Us Now" at some of their sold-out concerts. Here, they perform at the MGM Grand Garden Arena in Las Vegas.

ANSWERS
1. c 2. d 3. a 4. b 5. c 6. a 7. b 8. d 9. b 10. c

CHAPTER 8
Joey Fatone

FULL NAME:

JOSEPH ANTHONY FATONE, JR.

(PRONOUNCED FA-TONE; THE "E" IS SILENT)

BORN:

JANUARY 28, 1977, IN BROOKLYN, NEW YORK

HOROSCOPE SIGN:

AQUARIUS

VITAL STATISTICS:

BROWN EYES, DARK BROWN HAIR

FAMILY:

PARENTS, PHYLLIS AND JOE FATONE, SR.; OLDER

SISTER, JANINE; OLDER BROTHER, STEVEN

PETS:

NONE

Joey has the brash, flirtatious manner that many associate with Brooklyn, which happens to be his hometown. You can picture him swaggering down the street in rhythm to an inner melody, like the John Travolta character in *Saturday Night Fever*. If Joey had to pick a character from a movie to play himself, though, he would choose the guy with the big red "S" on his chest. His obsession with Superman started when he was a child, when his attempts to fly often left him worse for wear—some of the scars still exist today.

Joey started collecting Superman memorabilia before he joined 'N SYNC, but his fans now associate him so much with it that, as he observed in an AOL chat, he is practically "Super Joey." "I have the symbol and the tattoo," he noted, adding, "I met Christopher Reeve and his wife and son in New Jersey. They came to see the show. This was after he had the accident. And his wife actually signed a picture for me, because she's authorized to sign his name. I was like—I couldn't even speak."

Joey showed promise as an actor at a young age, but his talent wasn't really singing—it was dancing. He learned jazz, tap, and modern dance, and honed his performing skills by acting in productions of *Music Man*, *Damn Yankees*, *Cyrano de Bergerac*, *Macbeth*, and *The Merchant of Venice*. In high school Joey also performed with three friends in a group called the Big Guys; like 'N SYNC, they specialized in harmonies.

Opposite: Joey's so excited about the sales of No Strings Attached *that he's literally kicking up his heels!*

Right: Twenty-three-year-old Joey Fatone's musical beginnings were greatly influenced by his father, who used to sing in a doo-wop group.

Joey's quest to be Superman may have been thwarted (rumor has it that Nicholas Cage has been cast in the upcoming remake) but he has earned some screen credits. When he was only fourteen, Joey got a part in the John Goodman movie *Matinee*, and soon afterward he was cast as a guest star in the science-fiction series *SeaQuest*. From there Joey moved on to a variety of roles at Universal Studios, Orlando, singing in a doo-wop band similar to the one his father had performed with and playing such characters as Dracula and the Wolfman. While he was at Universal, Joey met Chris Kirkpatrick—the rest, as they say, is history.

Joey enjoys touring and getting to see the world, but, as he told *J-14* magazine for a special 'N SYNC issue, "The best part of being on tour is meeting our fans and performing in front of thousands of people. It's a great feeling to touch so many lives."

Fan Christine Sinclair recalls a close encounter with Joey during the group's performance of "Sailing." "I whipped out my hand and waved to him, and he was so close to me that I could have touched his hand, but I was stupid at the time and didn't think of tippy toes," she explains. "Close but no Joey."

Left: Joey showing off his famous tongue.

Opposite: It doesn't matter if he's in a T-shirt and jeans or leather and khakis (as seen in this 1998 pic), Joey always manages to look good.

1. In an interview on BBC Online earlier this year, Joey mentioned a certain breakfast food that he likes but never gets to eat, because the other guys beat him to it. What food was it?
a. Krispy Kreme donuts
b. Frosted Flakes cereal
c. Chocolate Pop-Tarts
d. Lucky Charms cereal

2. Why is Joey wearing a beanie-type hat in most of the U.S. video of "I Want You Back"?
a. He had an eyebrow pierced so he could wear a ring in it, but it got infected.
b. He tried to dye his hair red and it started falling out in chunks.
c. Wearing the beanie was a secret message to a girl back home.
d. A fan gave him the beanie before they shot the video, and he just liked it.

3. Not too long ago, *J-14* magazine did a photo feature called "The Many _____ of Joey Fatone." Fill in the blank.
a. Moods
b. Faces
c. Tongues
d. Tattoos

4. When Joey was a child he appeared as an extra in which movie?
a. *PeeWee's Big Adventure*
b. *Once Upon a Time in America*
c. *The Princess Bride*
d. *Kindergarten Cop*

5. Who is Joey's favorite comedian?
a. Adam Sandler
b. Chris Farley
c. Howie Mandel
d. Billy Crystal

6. What kind of vehicle is Joey driving these days?
a. A black Cadillac truck
b. A silver Porsche Boxter
c. A red Plymouth Prowler
d. A chrome-yellow vintage Corvette

7. Joey has been quoted as saying he would love to play the lead in an upcoming film. What character does he want to play?
a. John Lennon
b. Bullwinkle Moose
c. Buddy Holly
d. Superman

8. The setting for which music video was Joey's idea?
a. "Tearin' Up My Heart"
b. "Bye Bye Bye"
c. "I Want You Back"
d. "I Drive Myself Crazy"

9. When asked about his favorite Superman collectible, Joey usually mentions a hand-knitted Superman sweater. But when 'N SYNC appeared live on MTV in March 2000, Joey said that this was his most treasured Superman item. What is it?
a. Christopher Reeve's autograph
b. The Superman costume he wore as a child
c. A GI Joe–type Superman doll
d. Issue no. 1 of the *Superman* comic book series

10. After high school, Joey got a job at Universal Studios, singing and dancing in which live show?
a. *Beauty and the Beast*
b. *Beetlejuice's Graveyard Revue*
c. *Blues Brothers Revue*
d. *Rocky Horror Show*

9. a 10. b

1. c 2. a 3. c 4. b 5. c 6. a 7. a 8. d

ANSWERS

Center: There's that big red "S" again, but Clark Kent must be sporting a new look these days!

Above: Joey hitting all the right notes at the Teen People First Anniversary Party held at the Key Club in Georgia.

Above: Just your average Superman: Joey Fatone.

Opposite: Joey in a thoughtful moment, looking serious and soulful.

CHAPTER 9

No Strings Attached to These Boys

For an American band—five hometown boys with boy-next-door roots—'N SYNC has soared as high or higher than any band in history. Rock' n' roll purists may scorn the so-called "boy bands" as manufactured pretty boys who can't sing, but that argument just doesn't hold up. First of all, each of the band members had musical or professional performing experience before 'N SYNC was even a twinkle in Chris Kirkpatrick's eye. They knew each other and several had performed together long before they were herded together under the "boy band" heading. No one disputes that they're good-looking, but being "the cute one" never kept Paul McCartney from getting the respect of the music world when *his* "boy band" performed.

So they don't play instruments? When was the last time Mick Jagger played lead guitar while he sang? And while many popular groups perform songs written by others, in fact, members of 'N SYNC have written some of their own songs. And as for their singing, every member of the band could stand alone on singing talent, but as it happens, they are equally talented as performers—a feat many rock 'n' rollers can't equal.

As performers and musicians, the members of 'N SYNC called their latest album *No Strings Attached* to emphasize that they are not boy band puppets—and for that matter, not boys any longer but young men with determination and talent. After inundating the airwaves with a monthlong marathon that had 'N SYNC doing guest shots on *Saturday Night Live*, the Grammy Awards, the Academy

Left: Let them eat cake! Getting ready to introduce face and cake at the First Annual Teen People *Anniversary Party.*

Opposite: Lance goes for the gold as the gang dons shiny duds for a party at FAO Schwartz, New York City.

Awww, shucks! JC strikes a shy pose for Music with a Message: World AIDS Day, in December 1999.

Awards, *The Rosie O'Donnell Show*, *The View*, *The Tonight Show with Jay Leno*, ABC's *Good Morning America*, Nickelodeon's *Snick House* and *All That*, and MTV's *TRL* and *'N SYNC TV*, in addition to a number of online interviews and promotional events celebrating the CD's release, you might think the guys would be ready to veg for a month or two. Not likely.

Kicking off a hotly anticipated U.S. tour in Biloxi, Mississippi, on May 9, the present schedule includes performances in fifty-two venues. And after that? Well, the rest of the world is waiting for its turn to see 'N SYNC live.

'N SYNC is also looking to the big screen in the future, with Lance Bass performing in the upcoming film *Jack of All Trades*, a movie produced by Lou Pearlman of TransContinental Records. Britney Spears and Kenny Rogers have roles in the film, and fans should watch for many cameos by celebrities, including the four other members of 'N SYNC.

The band members are anxious to get involved with other videos and big-screen films; they have even discussed some ideas with Tom Hanks. Already in production is a home movie to beat all home movies—a collection of never-before-seen snippets from each of the guy's own family home movies, including footage of the band's earliest performances. As Joey Fatone told MTV News, "It's everything from traveling to toboggan rides."

'N SYNC headed to Cannes in May, unveiling details of their new movie, which is scheduled to start shooting early next year. All the 'N SYNC members will have parts in the movie, produced by Total Film Group and the band's Phat Free Productions, but they will not play themselves.

Television, tours, movies, videos, and, we hope, many more CDs—just what else can they do to top this? Well, there's always the White House . . .

Above left: 'N SYNC charming the crowd at the 100th Birthday Blast concert for Pax at Radio City Music Hall in New York City.

Above: Chris performing at the MCI Center in Washington, D.C., March 19, 1999.

Surfin' for 'N SYNC on the Web

It's getting easier every day to find out anything about anybody online, and the Internet is certainly a good place to link up with other 'N SYNC fans, look for tour or CD information, or check out the latest gossip. Remember, though, that a lot of strange people hide behind the anonymity of the Web. Just because a Web site says something like "Lance Bass' Own Website" doesn't mean that Lance is involved with it, has authorized it, or even knows anything about it. While the guys in 'N SYNC do like to visit fan sites, chat rooms, and many sites related to music, this does not mean that you can believe it if someone has the screen name "JustiNsync" or something similar, and swears he is one of the band. It is never a good idea to give out your name, address, or phone number to people you have only met online, even if you really feel you could be soulmates or best friends.

At the time of this writing, the official N'SYNC website, www.nsync.com, has been updated and is finally up and running again. Finding a good site can be a problem, because many of the sites listed in older 'N SYNC books are no longer operational. Hundreds—even thousands—of fans have set up their own Web sites with 'N SYNC articles, fan fiction, tour reviews, contests, photos, and links to other sites. In addition to the many sites that sell official 'N SYNC merchandise, you can often find collector's items or great fan photos of the group on auction sites such as Amazon.com, Yahoo, and eBay.com (you may have to have a parent place your bid, though, because some auctions allow bidding only if you are eighteen or over).

If you are looking for specific information, try going to a search engine first. There are a lot of great search engines out there, and they don't cost anything to use. Just type in the name (www.google.com, for example) and then when the screen comes up, type in what you are looking for. Say you are looking for information on the sales figures for *No Strings Attached*. You would type in "Nsync, No Strings Attached" and hit "search" or "go." Sometimes it is easier to find something if you limit the search words to two, such as "Nsync, CD." Be sure to enclose your search words in quotation marks or the computer will list every item that includes the word "CD." The quotation marks mean that the computer will search for only those items that contain both of those words. Here are some of the best search engines:

www.google.com
www.excite.com
www.yahoo.com
www.snap.com
www.altavista.com
www.infoseek.com
www.hotbot.com
www.lycos.com
www.askjeeves.com
www.goto.com
www.alltheweb.com
www.looksmart.com
www.northernlight.com
www.webcrawler.com
www.directhit.com

Narrowing down the search is another story. For instance, a quick search on the word "Nsync" at Altavista.com brought up 42,435 hits. You can narrow it down by searching for your favorite, but remember that the majority of the hits will be fan sites. There is nothing wrong with that, except that they might not contain reliable information. The biggest problem with fan sites is that they seem to come and go very quickly. Check out the following sites for up-to-date 'N SYNC info:

www.nsync.com (official site)
fumanskeeto.com (Chris Kirkpatrick's clothing site)
www.nsyncworldwide.com (formerly crunk)
www.peeps.com/nsync2 (**Note:** www.byebyebye.com will also take you to this site)
www.nsyncworld.com
nso.hypermarket.net/nsyncinfo.html (discography)
www.surf.to/nsynctown (This site was created by a teenage Malaysian girl who has kept it up to date for at least two years.)
www.casenet.com/people/nsync.htm
www.celebrityscreensavers.com/nsync.html (free screen saver)
www.n-sync.de/bilder_frameset.html (German Jive site)
www.nsyncstudio.com
wallofsound.go.com/artists/nsync/content/news.html
geocities.com/nsyncfandom/factoids.html
www.gurlpages.com/music
datworld.com/music/pop/nsync
www.billboard.com
www.mtvnews.com
www.cdnow.com
rollingstone.tunes.com
www.nsync.de/english/music/0002.html (BMG German 'N SYNC discography)
CDWorld.com, Amazon.com (additional discography)

'N SYNC 'n concert: They can say "Bye Bye Bye" a million times but their fans aren't going anywhere! And with Billboard reporting one million tickets bought the first day of sales for their fifty-two-show tour (bringing in close to $40 million), it looks like they will be playing sold-out concerts for some time to come.

Sailing, takes me away . . . but, hey, where's our boat? "It's about this long, and this wide," Joey and JC seem to be saying.

Sources

'N Sync Official Fan Club publications and newsletter

PUBLICATIONS

Bander, David. (AP) "'N SYNC's New Disc Doubles Sales Record." *Cincinnati Enquirer*, March 30, 2000.

Laudadio, Marisa, and Ellen Lieberman. "'N SYNC Inside and Out: The Sky's the Limit." *TEEN*, April 2000, pp. 16, 54–60, 72–73.

"Life Story." 'N SYNC Special Collectors Edition, *J-14*, Fall 1999.

Netter, Matt. *'N SYNC: Tearin' Up the Charts*. New York: Archway Paperbacks, Simon & Schuster, 1998.

———. *'N SYNC with Justin*. New York: Archway Paperbacks, Simon & Schuster, 1999.

Neumaier, Joe. "'N SYNC: Back 'N Action." *Disney Adventures*, March 2000, pp. 35–43.

Nichols, Angie. *'N SYNC Confidential*. London: Virgin Publishing, 1999.

'N SYNC, with K. M. Squires. *'N SYNC: The Official Book*. New York: Dell Books for Young Readers, 1998.

"'N SYNC on the Court." *Pop Star*, January–February 2000, pp. 13–19.

"Partying with 'N SYNC." *J-14*, February 2000, pp. 28–31; also miscellaneous. news items, pp. 18, 19.

Williams, Jeannie. "Academy Awards Singing Gig Has 'N SYNC Boys Agog." *USA Today*, March 23, 2000.

INTERNET ARTICLES

"The Giving Back Fund Joins Justin Timberlake at White House Conference on Philanthropy," and "'N SYNC's Justin Timberlake Joins with The Giving Back Fund to Start Charitable Foundation." Press releases, http://givingback.digistar.com/newsite/media, October 1999.

"Jenison, David. "'Nother Week at No. 1 for 'N SYNC," aol.eonline.com/news, April 26, 2000.

"'N SYNC, Joe, Make Jive Proud," www. billboard.com/daily April 2000.

"'N SYNC, Notorious B.I.G. Hit Diamond Sales," www.mtv.com/news/gallery, February 3, 2000.

"'N SYNC, Ready to Unveil New Film Project at Cannes," www.mtv.com/news, April 2000

"'N SYNC's, Lance Gets Good Ankle News," www. mtv.com/news/headlines, March 14, 2000.

"'N SYNC's, Money Making Meal," www.bbc.co.uk/radio1/news/music/000310_nsync.html, March 21, 2000.

Smith, Courtney. "'N SYNC's Lance Puckers Up for '7th Heaven,'" www.mtv.com/news/gallery, January 21, 2000.

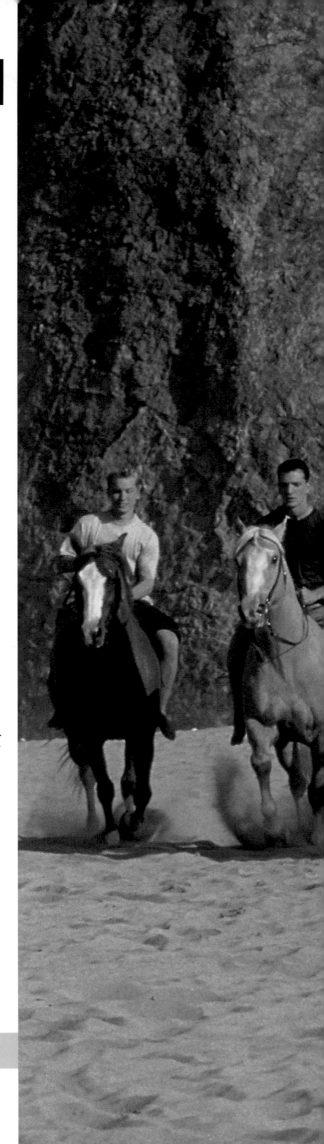

Wild horses: Shooting "For the Girl . . ." in 1998.

Index

Albums, 67–68, 72–73

Bass, Lance, *8*, 13, 44, 56–58, *56–59*,
    61. *61–63*, 86
Brooks, Garth, 44

"Challenge for the Children," 44
Charities, 44–45, 50
Chasez, JC, *9*, 10, *10*, 11, *12*, 26, *26–35*, 27, 29–30
ChildWatch, 45
Clapton, Eric, 44
Clinton, Hillary, 45, 50
Crow, Sheryl, 44

Defeo, Jack, 58

Early years, 10–13
Edwards, Meredith, 58
Estefan, Gloria, 44, 67

Fans, 14–15, 21, 29–30, *36*, 38–41,
    40–41, 50, 61, 78
Fatone, Joey, *9*, 10, *10*, 11, 44, 76–78, *76–83*, 87
"Feed the World," 45
Free Lance Entertainment, 58
FuMan Skeeto, 17–18

Giving Back Fund, 45, 50

Hanks, Tom, 86
Harless, Lynn, 11

Irazarry, Ron, 17

Jack of All Trades, 86
Justin Timberlake Foundation, 45, 50

Kirkpatrick, Chris, *9*, 10, *10*, 11, 16–18,
   16–25, 21, 45, 78
Kravitz, Lenny, 44

"Let the Music Heal Your Soul," 45

Matinee, 78
Mickey Mouse Club, The 10–11, *12*, 49
Millennium, 68
Model Behavior, 45–46
Movies, 45–46, 78, 86–87
Music and Media Catalogue, 72–73
"Music of My Heart," 57, 67

Naming of band, 11–13
No Strings Attached, 8, 27, 49, 67–68, 72, 84

Paltrow, Gwyneth, 44
Pearlman, Lou, 8

Quizzes, 13, 22, 33, 46–47, 53, 60, 74–75, 80–81

Rogers, Kenny, 86

"Save the Music," 44
SeaQuest, 78
Spears, Britney, 86
Sting, 45
Superman, 77

Team Harmony VI, 44–45
7th Heaven, 57–58
Timberlake, Justin, *8, 10,* 10–11, *12,* 44,
   45, 48–50, *48–55*

Websites, 88–89

Photo Credits